Bill Fletcher

Great Scottish Discoveries and Inventions

Illustrated by John Harrold

Richard Drew Publishing, Glasgow

✳✧✳✧✳✧✳✧✳✧✳✧✳✧✳✧✳✧✳✧✳✧✳✧✳✧✳✧✳✧✳

✳✧✳✧✳✧✳✧✳✧✳✧✳✧✳✧✳✧✳✧✳✧✳✧✳✧✳✧✳✧✳

British Library Cataloguing in Publication Data

Fletcher, Bill
Great Scottish discoveries and inventions.
1. Science — Scotland — History
I. Title
509'.411   Q127.S3
ISBN 0-86267-085-3
ISBN 0-86267-084-5 Pbk

First Published 1985 by Richard Drew Publishing Ltd,
6 Clairmont Gardens, Glasgow G3 7LW
Reprinted 1986

Designed by James W Murray
Printed and bound in Great Britain
Set in Raleigh by John Swain Ltd, Glasgow

The Steam Engine
JAMES WATT (1736—1819)

When James Watt went for a year to London to train as an instrument maker, it took him twelve days on horseback to get there from his home in Greenock. His master, John Morgan, charged him a fee of 20 guineas and James had to work until 9 o'clock every night except Saturday. He tried to live on eight shillings a week, including his board and lodgings, so that he would not be too great a financial strain on his father. He was afraid to go out at night for there were more than forty 'press gangs' roaming London who seized all able-bodied men that they could lay their hands on and put them into the Navy, which was desperately needing men for the Seven Years War with France. They were known to 'press' or capture a thousand men in one night. There were also agents for the East India Company, who kidnapped men and drafted them into the Indian Army. No wonder Watt did not enjoy his stay in London! He was glad to get back to Greenock.

After a short spell at home he went to Glasgow to set up in business as an instrument maker. Then he found to his surprise that he wasn't allowed to do so. The Incorporation of Hammermen in Glasgow, who decided such matters in those days, told him that he was banned because he was neither the son of a Glasgow citizen, nor was he trained in Glasgow.

Fortunately, Glasgow University came to his rescue and offered him the chance of opening a shop within the University, to make instruments for the Science and Engineering departments and to repair any machines that went wrong. In his spare time he made fiddles, flutes, guitars and organs. In the University James became friendly with some famous professors, including Joseph Black, Professor of Chemistry, from whom he learned much about the properties of heat. Another professor, John Anderson, one day gave Watt a steam engine to repair.

The engine was named after its inventor, Newcomen. Watt decided that it was not a very efficient kind of engine. One Sunday morning in the spring of 1765, when he was walking in Glasgow Green, he suddenly thought of a way in which he could improve the

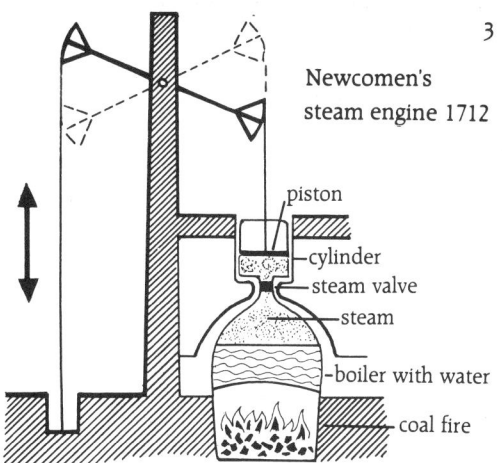

Newcomen's steam engine 1712

Newcomen engine. He hurried back to his workshop in the University. There, he made a model to try out his idea. He found that the new engine he had invented worked about ten times better than Newcomen's.

However, a long period of difficulty and disappointment lay ahead. He could not find an engineering firm which could make a piston exact enough to fit the cylinder so that steam did not escape and make his engine ineffective. He spent much of his own money in trying to perfect his engine, and he fell into debt. He had to put aside this work and he got a job as a civil engineer. He was good at this work too — during this time he built the Monkland Canal on which barges would carry coal from the Lanarkshire pits to Glasgow.

Later, Watt joined the great manufacturer Matthew Boulton in Birmingham. Between them they made Watt's engine and improved it still further. Orders for the steam engine came from all over the world and it was used to drive machinery in cotton and grain mills, to press out metal coins, to mine coal and lead and tin, and in breweries and distilleries.

For centuries, the people of Britain had worked mainly on the land, growing crops and rearing farm animals. In the 17th century, however, immigrants came to Britain from Europe, bringing with them skills in making watches and clocks, paper, glass and mechanical toys. Soon these skills spread among the British people, but the manufacturing was done at home in their own cottages. Later, machines were invented to do some of the work. Factories were built near rivers, so that water-power could be used to drive the machines. When Watt invented his steam engine, it soon replaced water-power. Coal was used to heat the steam, which led to the opening up of the coalfields of Britain. Instead of working in their cottages, people flocked into the huge factories in the industrial cities that grew up near the coalfields. This change is sometimes referred to as the Industrial Revolution.

Britain became the greatest industrial nation in the world, and her wealth and her prosperity were mainly due to Watt's invention.

The Newcomen engine worked by heating water in a vessel to form steam. As the steam expanded, it raised a piston in the vessel. Water was then led into the vessel to cool the steam. The steam contracted, forming a vacuum, and the piston fell to its original position. The water was heated again: steam formed and raised the piston. This process was repeated again and again.

Watt realised that this was not a very efficient system because the cold water, as well as cooling the steam, cooled the vessel. So, instead of cooling the steam in the vessel, he let it escape into a separate container, or condenser, as he called it. This created the vacuum in the vessel and the piston fell. The water in the separate condenser was reheated and entered the vessel as steam, raising the piston again.

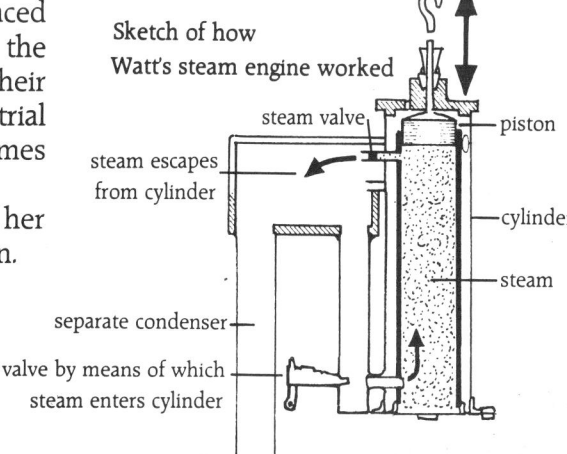

Sketch of how Watt's steam engine worked

The Pioneer of Technical Education
PROFESSOR JOHN ANDERSON (1726–1796)

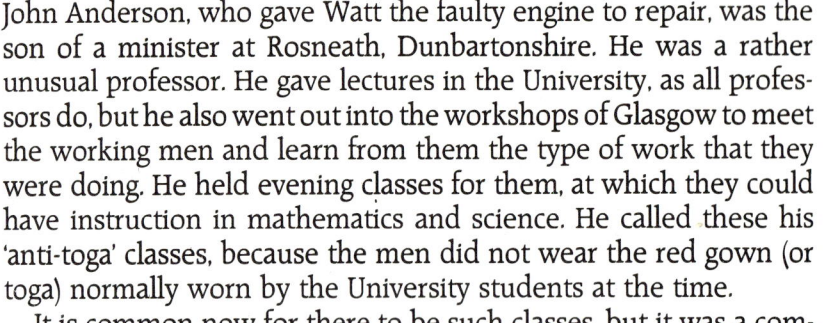

John Anderson, who gave Watt the faulty engine to repair, was the son of a minister at Rosneath, Dunbartonshire. He was a rather unusual professor. He gave lectures in the University, as all professors do, but he also went out into the workshops of Glasgow to meet the working men and learn from them the type of work that they were doing. He held evening classes for them, at which they could have instruction in mathematics and science. He called these his 'anti-toga' classes, because the men did not wear the red gown (or toga) normally worn by the University students at the time.

It is common now for there to be such classes, but it was a completely new idea in the 18th century and Anderson was probably the first man in Britain to hold them. The classes were so successful that over two hundred workmen regularly attended his lectures. However, his success did not make him very popular with his fellow professors at Glasgow University. He had many arguments with them and because of his fiery temper they called him 'Jolly Jack Phosphorus'.

As a young man he had gone to live with an aunt in Stirling when his father died. When he was only 19 he was in charge of a band of soldiers raised to defend Stirling against the army of Bonnie Prince Charlie. Later, he invented a new kind of field gun — John Paul Jones, the Scotsman from Kirkcudbright who founded the navy of the United States of America, came to inspect it. Anderson offered his gun to the British Government. When they showed no interest in it, he offered it to the French instead. They gave it a place of honour and put an inscription on it, 'The Gift of Science to Liberty', but they do not appear to have manufactured it for use in war. Anderson also suggested to the French government that they should use balloons, made of paper and varnished with boiled oil, to carry propaganda across the lines of the German army, who were their enemies. But later, when there was fear of a French invasion of Britain, he helped to fortify Greenock, which was one of the most important ports to the country.

Anderson's main interest, however, was in the education of the working man and when he died he left instructions that his money

was to be used to start a new university — Anderson's University — which would be run, not by the professors, but by representatives from trade and industry. The job of the professor would be to provide instruction in arts, science and engineering subjects, not only to men, but also to women. Unfortunately John Anderson did not leave any money, but within a year of his death the trustees of his estate had raised enough to open Anderson's Institution (later Anderson's University) in 1796. In the first session there were 972 students, about half of whom were women. Today, after numerous changes of title, Anderson's Institution is the University of Strathclyde, with more than 6000 students.

It was Anderson who saw the need for well-educated, well-trained mechanics and artisans and who, by his example, provided the workmen ready to take advantage of the Industrial Revolution which followed Watt's invention of his steam engine. He was the first person to try to provide technical education and to bring scientific learning within the reach of everyone.

Lighting up the World With Gas
WILLIAM MURDOCH (1754–1839)

In Scotland in the middle of the 18th century there was not much opportunity for young men to develop their abilities in Industry. So at the age of 24, William Murdoch set out to walk from the little village of Auchinleck in Ayrshire, where he was born, to find employment with Boulton and Watt at their Soho works in Birmingham. William's father was a mill-owner, and as well as sending his son to the village school, he had also taught him engineering, woodwork and stonemasonry. So it was a very talented young man who was interviewed by Mr Boulton himself, and when he also explained that he had made, on his father's turning machine, the circular stove-pipe hat which he was wearing, Boulton employed him on the spot. He was sent to Cornwall to look after the engines which had been installed by Watt to pump water out of the tin mines. He had also to collect the rents for the use of the engines from the Cornish mine owners, or 'mine-captains' as they were called.

This was no easy task, but he soon earned people's respect. Every time the engines broke down, and it looked as if the mines would be flooded, it was Murdoch who went in and repaired them. He also made many improvements in Watt's engine. The mineworkers soon recognised that they had a friend among them whose mechanical ability amounted almost to genius. He married a Cornish girl and settled down happily at his home in Redruth. Since the English had difficulty in pronouncing his name properly, he changed it to Murdock.

In his spare time he built a little steam locomotive using Watt's engine to provide power. He tried it out one summer evening on the long avenue leading to the parson's house. Unfortunately, he nearly scared the wits out of the parson who, seeing the hissing, fiery little machine approaching him, thought that it was the devil! However, Murdoch got little encouragement in this from Boulton or Watt: otherwise he, and not Stephenson, might have invented the first locomotive. Indeed, today there is a plaque on his house in Cornwall which states, 'William Murdock lived in this house 1782–1798, made the first locomotive here and tested it in 1784'.

He also continued experimenting with the production of gas from coal, in which he had been interested as a boy in Auchinleck. In 1792,

he laid gas pipes and lit up his house and office at Redruth. This was the first successful demonstration of a building being lit by gas lighting. He also lit up the front of the Soho works in Birmingham in brilliant fashion to celebrate the end of the war with France in 1802. He tried to persuade Boulton and Watt that this was a very important discovery and that he should take out a patent which would ensure that a large share of the profits from its development would come to the company. But Watt was not impressed and he and Boulton would not give support. Soon other companies started developing gas lighting, and its use spread all over Britain and far beyond. Watt later realised his mistake, especially when he came to Glasgow and found many of the factories there lit by gas.

In London, the 'London and Westminster Chartered Gaslight and Coke Company', under the management of a man trained by Murdoch at Soho, was authorised to light up London. Murdoch felt no bitterness about this. He remained a close friend of Boulton and Watt, staying on with the Soho Company, and when he died at the age of 85, he was buried beside Matthew Boulton and James Watt in the graveyard of the Parish Church at Handsworth, near Birmingham.

The Invention of Steam Ships

WILLIAM SYMINGTON (1763—1831)
PATRICK MILLER (1737—1825)
JAMES TAYLOR (1753—1825)
HENRY BELL (1767—1830)

Symington

No one knows who invented boats — that brave soul is lost in the mists of ancient times, but the first man to propel them by means of steam power was William Symington. He was born in Leadhills, Lanarkshire where his father was an engineman employed in super-intending one of Boulton and Watt's pumping engines at the lead mines at Wanlockhead. William's father wanted him to study for the ministry, but he was more interested in being an engineer. He built a model of a steam road carriage and showed this to the professors of Edinburgh University. They were impressed but Scottish roads were in such poor condition that the idea of running a steam carriage over them was quite impractical.

However, James Taylor, who was also born in Leadhills, was the tutor to the family of a wealthy man, Patrick Miller, who had an estate in Dalswinton, Dumfriesshire. Taylor knew that Miller was interested in boats and had been experimenting with the possibility of hand-driven paddle steamers. He suggested to Miller that he should get Symington to fit an engine to one of his boats and turn the paddles in this way. Miller agreed. The first steamship in the world chugged across Dalswinton Loch at 5 mph in October, 1788. It is likely

First steamship on Dalswinton Loch

that the famous Scottish poet, Robert Burns, and the Scottish painter, Alexander Nasmyth were on the boat on this historic occasion.

Unfortunately, after a time Miller lost interest in developing the invention and nothing further was done about it for ten years. Then Lord Dundas, who was a governor of the Forth and Clyde Canal Company, suggested to Symington that instead of his barges being pulled by horses, it would be much better if they had paddles driven by a steam engine. Dundas built a beautiful barge which he named the 'Charlotte Dundas', after his daughter, and Symington fitted it out with an engine. It was a great success. The boat, towing two barges, travelled 19½ miles to Port Dundas in Glasgow against a strong headwind in six hours. However, the owners of the Canal were afraid that the waves from the paddles would wash away the banks of the canal and so all further experiments were stopped. An order for six steam paddle barges from England was also cancelled.

Symington was a very sad and disappointed man. He had spent all his money on these trials. He drifted to London and he died there on 22 March 1831. But his ideas did not die. Among the visitors who inspected the 'Charlotte Dundas' was Robert Fulton, an American artist. He got an engine from Boulton and Watt and launched his vessel 'Clermont' on the Hudson River in 1807.

Another man who knew of Symington's work was Henry Bell, who was born in Linlithgow in 1767 and who later moved to Helensburgh. His uncle gave him a present of a sailing model of a full-rigged ship when he was a schoolboy, and he spent many hours sailing it on the River Avon. From then on he was always interested in ships and while in Helensburgh he got a Port Glasgow shipyard to build him a boat which he fitted with a 3 horse-power engine. This was the 'Comet' and it plied between Glasgow and Greenock until 1820, when it was wrecked. It was the forerunner of the many great steamships that were to be built on, and sail from, the Clyde across the seven seas.

Charlotte Dundas

Bell

Comet

The Making of Britain's Roads
JOHN MACADAM (1756—1836)

When John Macadam — he later changed his name to McAdam, was a little boy at school in Maybole, Ayrshire, he showed an early interest in roads by making a model of the roadway between Maybole and Kirkoswald. He had, however, to wait many years before he could put his skills to practical use.

His father was a very rich man, but he lost all his money when the Ayr Bank, which he had established ten years before, collapsed and John, who had nine older sisters and brothers, went at the age of 14 to join his Uncle William in New York. Uncle William was a rich merchant engaged in shipping and he welcomed the young boy into his home and into his business.

John remained with his uncle for 13 years, during which the business thrived. Together, they founded the New York Chamber of Commerce with William as President and John as treasurer; and when John married a very wealthy American lady, it looked as if he would not return to his native land.

Then came the War of Independence. America, which had been a British colony, broke away from Britain. John, his uncle and his wife's family all supported Britain, and they lost most of the money that they had invested in America.

At the age of 29, John came back to Scotland. He bought an estate called Sauchrie, near Ayr, where he did road-making experiments at his own expense. He continued his experiments when he later moved to Bristol. They were so successful that he was appointed General Surveyor of Roads for the Bristol area. At this time the roads all over Britain were in a deplorable condition — loose and rough, dusty in dry weather and terribly muddy when it was wet. People seldom moved out of their own town or village. John Macadam changed all that with his new system of roadmaking.

The Bristol roads were so good that Macadam's fame spread all over Britain and he travelled thousands of miles every year explaining his system in different places. Soon he had so much work that he could not cope with it, so he sent for his three sons, who gave up their jobs in Scotland to become road surveyors too. Between them they transformed the road network of Britain and Macadam's roads were copied all over the world.

In his later life, John Macadam loved to pay summer and autumn visits to Scotland, to see the scenes of his boyhood. He travelled in a closed carriage drawn by two horses. Hitched on behind was a Newfoundland dog and a bridled pony. The dog's duty was to see the pony did not lag behind the coach! When Macadam came to places of interest — a glen, a castle or a road, he stopped the coach and rode off for a short spell on his pony. On returning from one of these Scottish trips he died, aged 80, at Moffat, Dumfriesshire. He was buried there, beside his grandmother.

Before Macadam, roads were made of earth, clay or chalk, which absorbed water. Macadam said that instead they should be of pieces of stone (preferably granite) which would be small enough to go through a two-inch ring — he gave workmen rings of this size to work with. The stones were scattered to a depth of ten inches. Under pressure of traffic, the sharp angles of the stones united to form a compact mass.

The road was laid with just enough rise in the centre to allow the rain to run off. Macadam said that it did not matter what weight the vehicle was that passed over it — indeed, the heavier the vehicle, the better: and the more traffic that ran over the road, the more compact it would become.

Dyes and Mackintoshes
CHARLES MACKINTOSH (1766–1843)

Charles Mackintosh of Glasgow started off his working life as a clerk, but he soon got a bit tired of that. He had devoted all his spare time to the study of chemistry and he was delighted when he got the chance to join his father's manufacturing chemist's business.

One of the main products of the works was called cudbear and in its day it was a well-known dye for silk and wool. It was prepared by mashing up lichen plant, which was got mainly from the Highlands of Scotland, in wooden troughs with ammonia and lime. The quality of the ammonia used was very important and Mackintosh believed that the best for his purpose was got from human urine. In those days there were no water toilets in the homes of the people — even the very rich had none, and Mackintosh sent his men round the houses of Glasgow, where they collected as much as 3000 gallons each day. The urine was then heated and the ammonia distilled off. Depending upon the proportions of the various elements that were used, the cudbear produced beautiful shades of pink, red, purple and blue. It was used throughout the world. It is not surprising that Mackintosh did everything in his power to hide the secrets of his manufacturing process. He built ten-foot walls round his factories and all the workmen that he employed were Highlanders whose only language was Gaelic, so that they could not pass on secrets to his competitors!

The end of the cudbear trade came about, not because of a shortage of lichen or of urine, but simply because of a change in fashion. Instead of wearing bright clothes, men and women started wearing clothes of grey and black. Everything was black — black hats, black suits and dresses, black shoes and stockings; even the carriages and coaches were black and so were the fireplaces and cooking pots. No one has ever been able to explain why this was so. Perhaps it was because they were living in an atmosphere of coal, iron and soot. The Mackintosh cudbear works closed in 1852.

But this was not the end of Mackintosh. He had turned his thoughts to rubber. It was the Spaniards who had noticed rubber during their conquests in South America and they brought some back to Europe. Unfortunately no one could find a use for it — it was just a hard lump. People tried to dissolve it in turpentine and ether but without success. Then Dr James Syme, Professor of Surgery in Edinburgh, suggested that naphtha might do the trick. So Charles Mackintosh bought up the tar which was a useless by-product in Murdoch's gas works in Glasgow, and by a special process got naphtha from it. He dissolved the rubber in naphtha to make a gluey substance and then used it to stick two pieces of cloth together. The cloth was now waterproof because the rubber solution filled the pores of the cloth and did not allow water to be absorbed. Instead it ran off. The raincoat or 'mackintosh' was born.

Mackintosh took out a patent for the process and set up factories in Glasgow and Manchester, turning out coats, capes, inflatable goods, cushions, pillows and beds. The company prospered and Charles Mackintosh became a very rich man. One thing did worry him, however, and that was the development of the railway system. He was afraid that since people did not now have to travel on horse-back and on the outside of stagecoaches, they might not need water-proof clothing. There may have been a slight fall-off in demand, but it was temporary. The British weather saw to that!

The Pneumatic Tyre
JOHN BOYD DUNLOP (1840−1921)

John Macadam's method of roadmaking had opened up the roadways of the world for travel. The mailcoach and the stagecoach carried people beyond their own little villages, and inns, where people might stay, sprang up all over Britain. Travel, however, was laborious and painful, for all sorts of vehicles were fitted with solid wooden or metal wheels. Among such vehicles was the bicycle, which had been invented by Kirkpatrick Macmillan, a blacksmith at Keir, Dumfriesshire. Macmillan built the first bicycle, with front-wheel steering and the rear wheels driven by pedals. In 1842 he made a cycling trip from his village to Glasgow. It took two days and he confessed that he was rather sore at the end of it.

Another Scot, John Boyd Dunlop, later provided the solution. He was born in Dreghorn, Ayrshire. His family were farmers, but John was not very strong so they sent him to Edinburgh University to become a vet. After qualifying, he set up practice in Belfast where he was very successful. His little son Johnny was a keen cyclist, but he complained to his father that he couldn't go as fast as he would like and beat his pals. Could his father do anything to speed up his tricycle? Father could and did. After thinking about the problem for a time, he realised that if he could make inflatable, bouncy tyres, then this would make greater speed possible. So he bent three strips of elmwood into hoops of about 3 ft in diameter and riveted the ends together. He made three rubber air tubes, covered them with canvas bags then with sheet rubber, inflated them and fitted them to the wheels of Johnny's tricycle. 'I told him to ride it over my newly laid

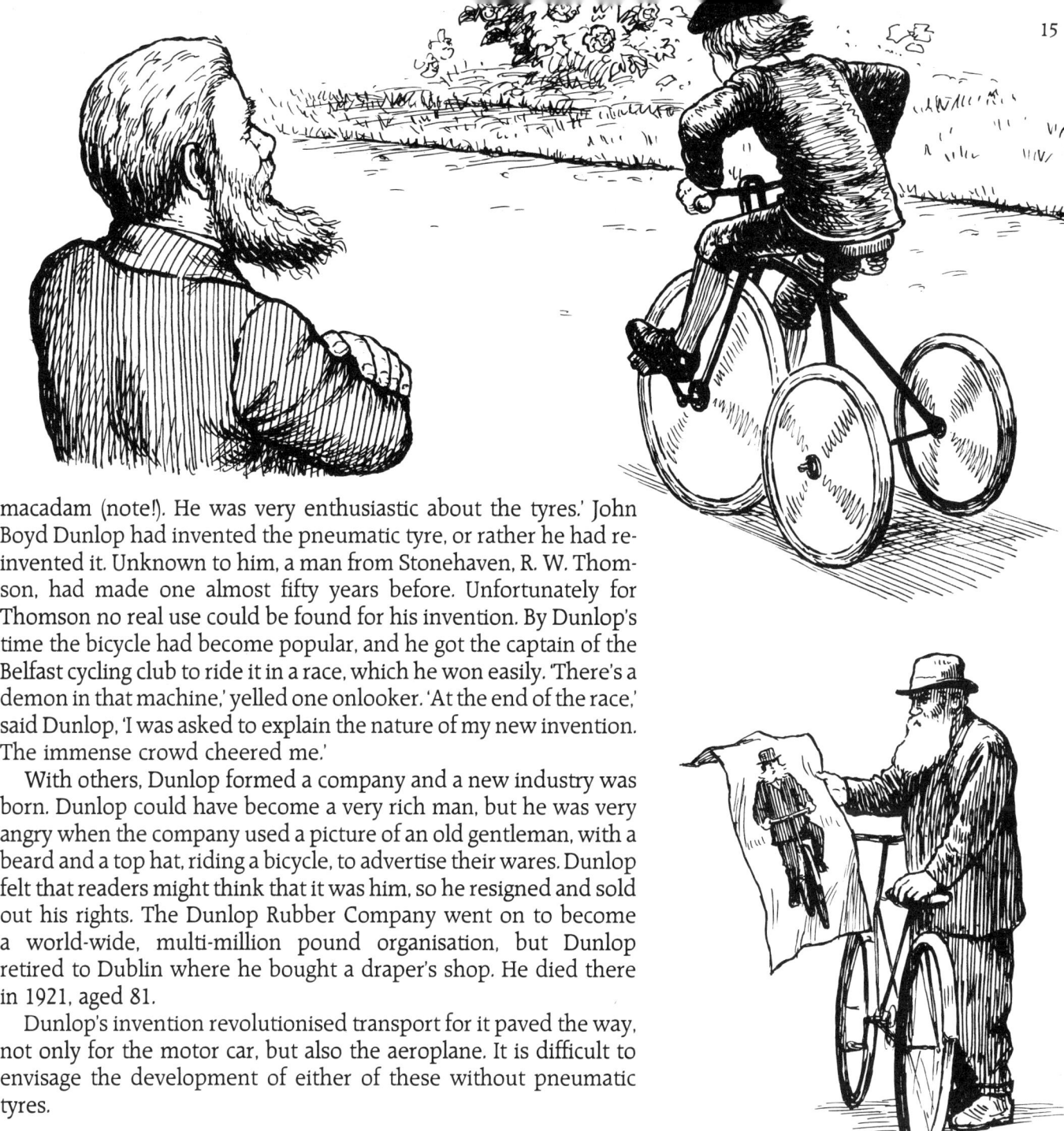

macadam (note!). He was very enthusiastic about the tyres.' John Boyd Dunlop had invented the pneumatic tyre, or rather he had re-invented it. Unknown to him, a man from Stonehaven, R. W. Thomson, had made one almost fifty years before. Unfortunately for Thomson no real use could be found for his invention. By Dunlop's time the bicycle had become popular, and he got the captain of the Belfast cycling club to ride it in a race, which he won easily. 'There's a demon in that machine,' yelled one onlooker. 'At the end of the race,' said Dunlop, 'I was asked to explain the nature of my new invention. The immense crowd cheered me.'

With others, Dunlop formed a company and a new industry was born. Dunlop could have become a very rich man, but he was very angry when the company used a picture of an old gentleman, with a beard and a top hat, riding a bicycle, to advertise their wares. Dunlop felt that readers might think that it was him, so he resigned and sold out his rights. The Dunlop Rubber Company went on to become a world-wide, multi-million pound organisation, but Dunlop retired to Dublin where he bought a draper's shop. He died there in 1921, aged 81.

Dunlop's invention revolutionised transport for it paved the way, not only for the motor car, but also the aeroplane. It is difficult to envisage the development of either of these without pneumatic tyres.

The World's First Oil Man

JAMES 'PARAFFIN' YOUNG (1811—1883)

The first oil well in the world was in Derbyshire in England. It was discovered by one Scotsman, developed by another one and it led to the establishment of a huge oil industry near Bathgate, between Glasgow and Edinburgh.

James Young, from the Drygate, a street near Glasgow Cathedral, worked with his father as a carpenter. But he was always interested in science and at the age of 19 he started attending evening classes at the nearby Anderson's University (now the University of Strathclyde). He excelled in chemistry and at the end of two years his professor, Thomas Graham, appointed him as his assistant. James must have been a good teacher for when later he was leaving to go to England with his professor, who had been appointed Master of the Mint, his students presented James with a gold watch.

When he was at University, James had made many friends and it was one of these, Lyon Playfair, who told him that he had found a spring of oil in his father-in-law's estate at Alfreton, Derbyshire. James bought the well and was soon producing lubricants and illuminating oils for the nearby Manchester cotton mills.

The well soon dried up, however, and James turned his thoughts to producing oil from coal. He wrote to Hugh Bartholomew, another friend of his student days, who was manager of the Glasgow Gas Works. Hugh told James that there was a kind of coal called oil shale found in the Bathgate area, which the people used in little braziers to light their houses. James Young came back to Scotland, bought up much of the land which contained the oil shale and set up great extracting and manufacturing works in the area. At one time there were about 120 works, employing about 40,000 men, turning out lubricating oils, illuminating oils, candles, paraffin and many other products from the shale. In time he came to be known as James 'Paraffin' Young.

In order to extract the oil, the shale had to be ground down into very fine particles and then heated; after extraction there was much waste material. This was piled up in great bings and you can still see many of these today when you travel from Glasgow to Edinburgh by rail or road, though some of the material has been used recently to build the M8 motorway.

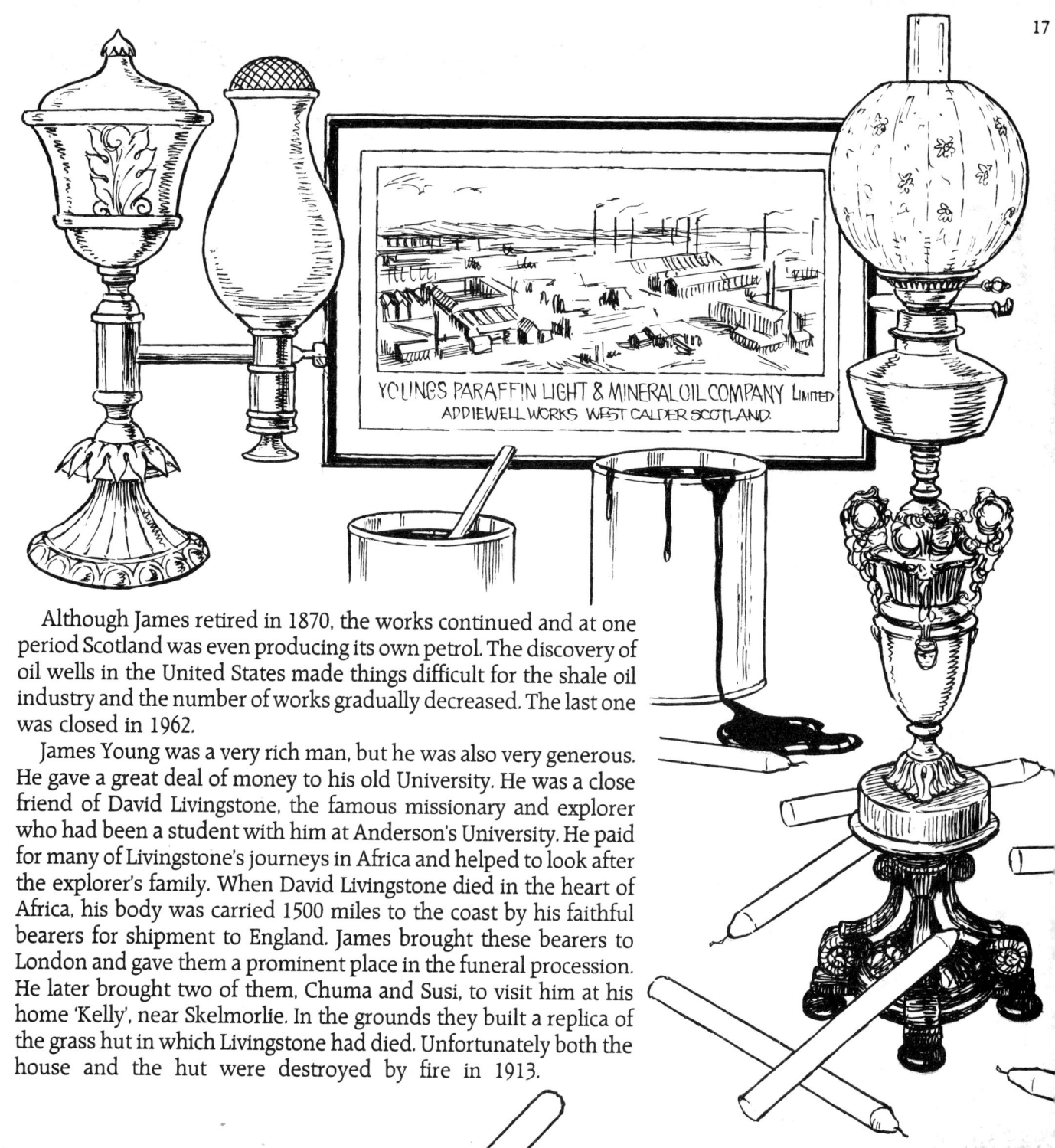

YOUNGS PARAFFIN LIGHT & MINERAL OIL COMPANY Limited
ADDIEWELL WORKS WEST CALDER SCOTLAND.

Although James retired in 1870, the works continued and at one period Scotland was even producing its own petrol. The discovery of oil wells in the United States made things difficult for the shale oil industry and the number of works gradually decreased. The last one was closed in 1962.

James Young was a very rich man, but he was also very generous. He gave a great deal of money to his old University. He was a close friend of David Livingstone, the famous missionary and explorer who had been a student with him at Anderson's University. He paid for many of Livingstone's journeys in Africa and helped to look after the explorer's family. When David Livingstone died in the heart of Africa, his body was carried 1500 miles to the coast by his faithful bearers for shipment to England. James brought these bearers to London and gave them a prominent place in the funeral procession. He later brought two of them, Chuma and Susi, to visit him at his home 'Kelly', near Skelmorlie. In the grounds they built a replica of the grass hut in which Livingstone had died. Unfortunately both the house and the hut were destroyed by fire in 1913.

The Transatlantic Cable
WILLIAM THOMSON — LORD KELVIN (1824 — 1907)

We can claim Lord Kelvin as a Scot, or at least share him with our Irish cousins. He was born in Belfast, but within the family there was a tradition that their forebears were Covenanters who had been 'rabbled out of Ayrshire by the Dragoons of Claverhouse in the 17th century' and had found refuge in Ulster. William's grandfather, his father and William himself all married Glasgow women and he had many relatives in that area. William's father had been a brilliant scholar at Glasgow University and after a spell as a professor in Belfast, he was appointed Professor of Mathematics in Glasgow. He brought his young son, William, eight years of age, with him.

William was brilliant too. He attended classes at the University when he was ten, winning many prizes and a medal. At the age of 17 he went to Cambridge and five years later, when only 22, he was appointed Professor of Natural Philosophy at Glasgow. He held the position for 53 years, although three times Cambridge University tried to entice him back there. In the first four years of his professorship he published 50 scientific papers, several of which were in French. Although many of his papers were of such a nature that non-scientists (and even some of his students!) could not understand them, they laid the foundations for many practical developments that were to follow much later, such as refrigeration and radio-communication.

Samuel Morse, an American, had invented a system of sending messages through wires by means of dots and dashes, called the 'Morse Code'. Both the British and the Americans used this system within their own countries. Now thoughts were turning to linking up the two countries by means of a transatlantic cable through which messages could be passed. Professor Thomson was put in charge of this difficult task. After a number of attempts and a number of failures due to the cable snapping, he succeeded in 1866. Now messages, which formerly took weeks by ship, could be transmitted in a few seconds. William Thomson was knighted by Queen Victoria. Meanwhile he continued to publish numerous scientific papers on a great variety of subjects and he travelled to many countries to give lectures.

Thomson was elected President of the Royal Society of London and Queen Victoria raised him to the peerage. He chose the title of Baron Kelvin of Netherhall, Largs — the Kelvin is the river that flows alongside Glasgow University in Kelvingrove Park and Netherhall was the name of his house in Largs on the Firth of Clyde, where he spent as much of his spare time sailing as he possibly could.

A few years later, King Edward VII elected him into the Order of Merit, when that Order was first instituted. The number of members is limited to 24.

When he had been a professor in Glasgow for 50 years, the occasion was duly celebrated by the City of Glasgow and by the University for two days, when guests from all over the world came to pay homage to him. Among them were kings and princes, statesmen and scientists from universities and learned societies.

When he resigned his professorship at the age of 75, he continued to write scientific papers, and he was made Chancellor of the University.

Many of Lord Kelvin's investigations have had, long after his death, very profound effects on our lives. His scientific work on energy and heat led to methods of air-conditioning in buildings and also to refrigeration and thus to the development of ice-cream and of frozen foods.

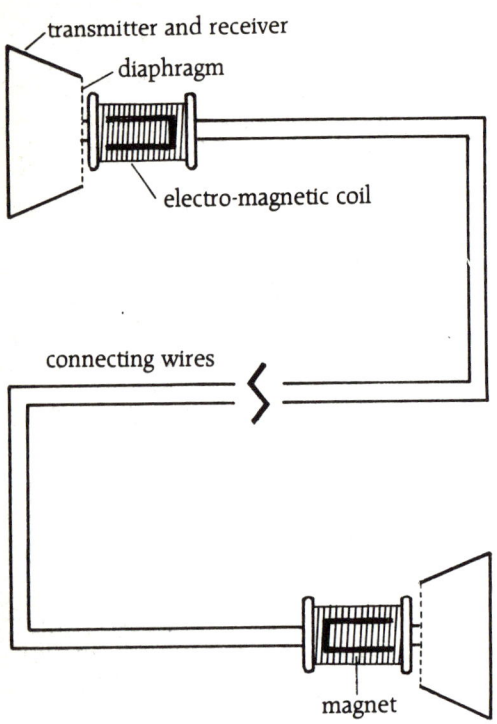

transmitter and receiver

diaphragm

electro-magnetic coil

connecting wires

magnet

Bell found that if the vibrations of air caused by human speech strike against a disc, they cause the disc (or diaphragm, as it is called) to vibrate. If the diaphragm is connected to a wire, then electric waves pass almost instantaneously along it. At the receiving end of the wire, the electric waves can be made to vibrate another diaphragm which reproduces the original sound. Note that the transmitter was also used as the receiver. Later the two were separated and improvements were made to the transmitter by Thomas Edison, the American inventor, and by a Yorkshire clergyman, R. Hunnings. Both these men introduced carbon granules behind the diaphragm. The carbon helped to convert the sound waves to electric current much more efficiently, and so messages could be sent over even longer distances.

The Telephone
ALEXANDER GRAHAM BELL (1847–1922)

When Alexander Graham Bell was a young man at university in Edinburgh, his native city, there was in the laboratory a piece of apparatus which had been made by a German schoolteacher named Philip Reis. It consisted of two boxes connected by an electric wire fed from a battery. If someone spoke or played a musical instrument into one of the boxes then a knitting needle which was suspended in the other began to vibrate and give off sounds resembling speech or music. Philip Reis called it a telephone. No one, however, took it very seriously. It was a curiosity.

When, however, Alexander moved with his mother and father to Canada, later becoming a teacher of vocal physiology at Boston in the USA, and married a young lady who had been deaf from birth, the memory of these boxes came back to him. Could he develop the idea and invent a hearing aid so that his wife and others could be rescued from their silent world?

Unfortunately the instrument he invented did not help deaf people to hear better, but by means of it sounds could be sent almost any distance in an instant. Remembering Philip Reis, Bell called his invention the telephone.

He had the device patented and then he demonstrated it at a big International Exhibition in Philadelphia. The Emperor of Brazil was there and when he held the receiver to his ear while Bell spoke into the transmitter at the other end of the hall, the Emperor nearly fell off his seat. 'Great Heavens,' he said, 'the thing talks'. Lord Kelvin, who was also in the party, said that it was 'one of the most interesting of the scientific inventions made in this century or that has ever been made in the history of science.'

Nevertheless, Bell had great difficulty in convincing people of the importance of his invention. He took his wife on holiday to England and took his telephones with him. A telephone wire was set up between the high steeple of Bow Church and the street below, and Londoners queued up and paid one penny to say, 'How do you do?' to a man on top of the steeple and hear him reply, 'Very well, thank you.' For Queen Victoria he set up a telephone connection between Osborne House on the Isle of Wight and Cowes, Southampton and

London. He installed a telephone in the gallery of the House of Commons and linked it to a newspaper office in Fleet Street so that the proceedings of the House could be reported immediately.

When Bell returned to America in 1878, he found that the first telephone exchange in the world had been set up in New Jersey with a hundred subscribers. A year later an exchange was set up in London and before long, telephones were to be found in every civilised country in the world. All were made to Bell's specification. The whole system of communication between people had been revolutionised.

Bell became a very rich man, but he took little further interest in the telephone. He lived in Canada and was seldom seen without his Tam o' Shanter bonnet and he made many visits to his beloved Scotland. He went back to teaching the deaf, but he had one great sadness. He was never able to make his beloved wife Mabel hear.

Television
JOHN LOGIE BAIRD (1888—1946)

John Logie Baird, who was born in Helensburgh on the Firth of Clyde, trained as an electrical engineer in the Royal Technical College (now the University of Strathclyde) in Glasgow. He was full of ideas, though unfortunately most of them didn't work, except for the most important one of all — television, and even with this one he was very unlucky.

He tried making artificial diamonds by passing an electrical current through a stick of carbon encased in concrete and nearly blew up Dalmarnock Power Station where he worked; he then invented medicated socks to 'keep the feet cool in summer and warm in winter'; he fell very ill and had to go to the warmer climate of Port of Spain to save his life, where he made chutneys and jams from the native fruits and sugar, but nobody wanted to buy them. Returning to Britain, he invented a glass razor blade which almost severed his jugular vein; and he had no more luck with pneumatic soled shoes which had balloons inside them.

Tired, sick, so thin as to be almost transparent, he was walking on the cliffs at Hastings when an idea came to him. Why not send pictures by wireless? And call it television.

The apparatus that Baird used was rather extraordinary — a tea chest, an old hat box, a lens from a bicycle lamp, sealing wax, glue, batteries and transformers, but he transmitted the shadow of a cardboard cross two feet across the room. He went on improving the apparatus with the help of £500 from his Scottish cousins.

On the 27 January 1926, he demonstrated his invention to forty scientists in the Royal Institution in London and in the same year the BBC carried out experimental transmissions from his attic. In the meantime Baird, using infra-red light, was able to transmit pictures of people sitting in total darkness. He named this 'Noctavision'.

In the following year, using a disc with three spirals of holes — one covered with a red coloured filter, one with blue and one with green, he invented colour television, which he demonstrated to the British Association for the Advancement of Science meeting in Glasgow University in 1928. He transmitted a television picture to the United States and he set up a company with a capital of £1 million to develop television. The BBC now carried out its first public transmission — about thirty people in the whole of the UK had receivers (bought from Baird's company). In 1931 Baird televised the Derby.

He was now at the height of his fame and he was fêted in USA. But other companies were in the market, particularly Marconi EMI, who used a system that was said to be superior to Baird's. After extended trials the BBC finally chose the Marconi system. Baird was bitterly disappointed. For a short time he experimented with big screen television in cinemas. When war broke out in 1939 all television was suspended for the duration. Before it really got going again, John Logie Baird had died.

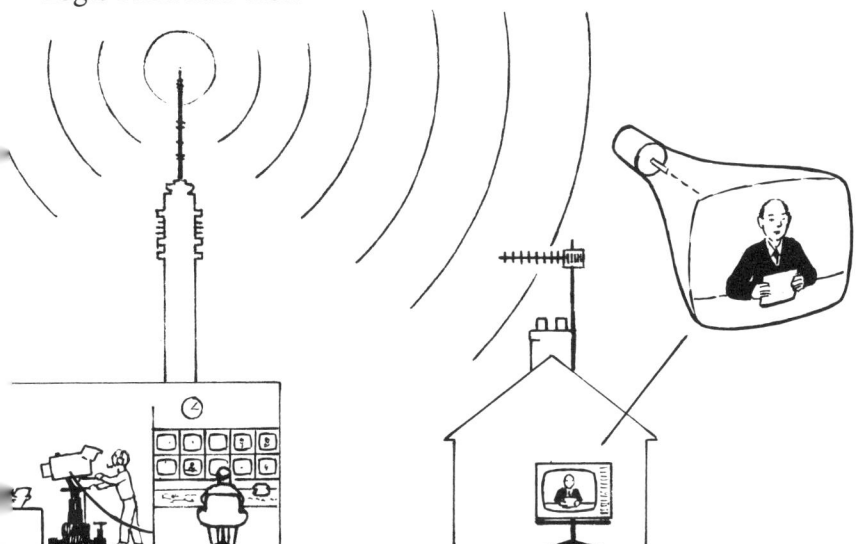

The way television works is that variations in light from an object produce electrical impulses in a photo-electric cell. These electrical impulses are magnified enormously by a valve. The impulses can be trapped by a radio receiver but instead of going through a loud-speaker, they are fed into a cathode ray tube. There they form tiny streams of electrons that impinge on a chemically-treated screen, on which the object is reconstituted by means of glowing dots.

Radar

ROBERT WATSON WATT (1902—1973)

In 1935 the British Government was worried about the possibility of war with Germany. When they asked Robert Watt if he could invent a 'death ray', he had to say that it was not possible. Instead he offered them radar, a system of locating an aeroplane even when enveloped in heavy cloud, even in total darkness, by means of radio waves. Radar was to save Britain in the 1939—45 war with Nazi Germany.

Watson Watt, born in Brechin and a graduate in engineering of the University College, Dundee, had entered the Royal Meteorological Office of the Royal Air Force as a scientist. He was involved in research into weather conditions and soon became deeply interested in radio waves. The Government asked him to investigate the possibility of being able to warn aircraft of impending thunder and lightning storms. He did this, but during his investigations he found out something much more important. If a radio beam was aimed at an aeroplane, then the beam was reflected back to Earth, thus indicating where the plane was. Watson Watt called this radio-location. Furthermore the length of time that it took for the wave to reach Earth, even though it was only a few millionths of a second, indicated exactly how far away the plane was.

The Air Ministry asked Watson Watt to demonstrate his invention to them. He did this in a small field in Daventry in Northamptonshire, and they were so impressed that they asked him to get a small team of scientists together to work on radio-location. They were so successful that it was decided, later in the year, to set up five radio-location stations on the east coast of England. By 1939, when war with Germany appeared certain, there was a continuous chain of radar stations (as they had come to be known) stretching from the north of Scotland to the Isle of Wight in England. In the summer of 1940, after conquering France, Germany sent great waves of aeroplanes over to bomb Britain into submission before invading with land forces. But the British defences were ready for them. Although the RAF had only a few hundred fighter planes, they were good ones and the young pilots were well trained. Furthermore the ground defence batteries and the aircraft were equipped with radar, which meant that they could locate the enemy early as he approached the

English Channel, and the British fighter planes could be directed to the enemy planes.

In the early stages the Germans attempted daylight raids, but so many of their aircraft were shot down that they changed to night bombing. They were no more successful with this, because even in the dark the British defences could locate enemy planes, using radar.

The Battle of Britain, as it was known, lasted from August to October. During it Germany lost 1733 aircraft, while Britain lost 915. Although the Germans continued afterwards to bomb Britain, they soon gave up all hope of invasion. Britain was saved, thanks to the quality of the aeroplanes, the bravery and ability of the pilots, and radar.

Radar is also used in peacetime. All airports in the world are fitted with it so that aircraft can be guided down. So too are all the major ports and harbours. Radar is being used to investigate the depths of the oceans, and in astronomy — to locate the stars in the Universe.

Robert Watson Watt was knighted for his work.

Chloroform

JAMES YOUNG SIMPSON (1811—1870)

When James Simpson, a baker's son from Bathgate, was a student at Edinburgh University, he almost gave up the study of medicine, so terrible were the sights that he had to endure in the operating theatres. There were no anaesthetics in those days, so that the patient had often to be dragged screaming to the theatre and held down by four or five men while the surgeon performed the operation with the patient fully conscious. Not only had the patient to endure terrible pain, but sometimes the shock of the operation killed him. Surgeons had to work fast.

James Simpson resolved that one day he would take the pain and terror out of operations and give surgeons time to work properly.

While he was still only a young man of 29 he was appointed Professor of Midwifery in the University. Midwifery is the study of childbirth. Professor Simpson soon became very famous, because he was not only a good doctor, he was a good lecturer too. Students flocked to his classes and wealthy and aristocratic patients — princesses, marchionesses and duchesses, came from all over Britain to consult him. He looked after the poor too and often did not send them a bill for his services. His fame was so great that Queen Victoria appointed him one of her physicians in Scotland.

Always before him, however, he had this picture of people having to suffer pain. If only he could put his patients to sleep so that they would wake up after the operation was over, having felt nothing! He had heard that ether was being used as an anaesthetic during surgical operations in Boston in USA. Simpson tried it himself, but he was not completely satisfied, for it had an unpleasant smell and it irritated the mouth and air passages.

Then it was suggested to him that he should try chloroform, which was used in chemical laboratories as a solvent. No doubt it had been noticed that when people sniffed it by mistake, they felt drowsy. Before using it on any patients, however, Simpson thought that he would try it out on himself and two of his assistant doctors. They sniffed the bottle, soon started snoring and fell into a deep sleep. This was a brave thing to do for they might have died. However, they didn't and they woke up some time later feeling fine.

A few days after this a little boy was operated on in the Royal Infirmary, having been given chloroform by Simpson. A large piece of diseased bone was cut out of his arm. He suffered no pain and he slept soundly all through the operation. There was, however, considerable opposition to its use — some said that Simpson was going against the will of God in trying to remove pain. Despite this it was widely used in the Crimean War and in the American Civil War, when more than 120 thousand operations were performed.

After Queen Victoria gave birth to her son, Prince Leopold, while anaesthetised, practically all opposition ceased. James Simpson was now the most famous surgeon in the world and honours were showered on him. Queen Victoria made him a baronet, Oxford University gave him an honorary degree and he was given the Freedom of Edinburgh.

When he was given the Freedom, he recalled how he had come to Edinburgh University as a poor lonely boy of 14 with a sack of oatmeal, a packet of oatcakes and a basket of eggs. His beloved mother had died when he was only eight, but his older brothers and sisters had rallied round, sacrificed what little money they had and supported 'Jamie' at University. He more than repaid their trust in him by helping to alleviate the pain of mankind.

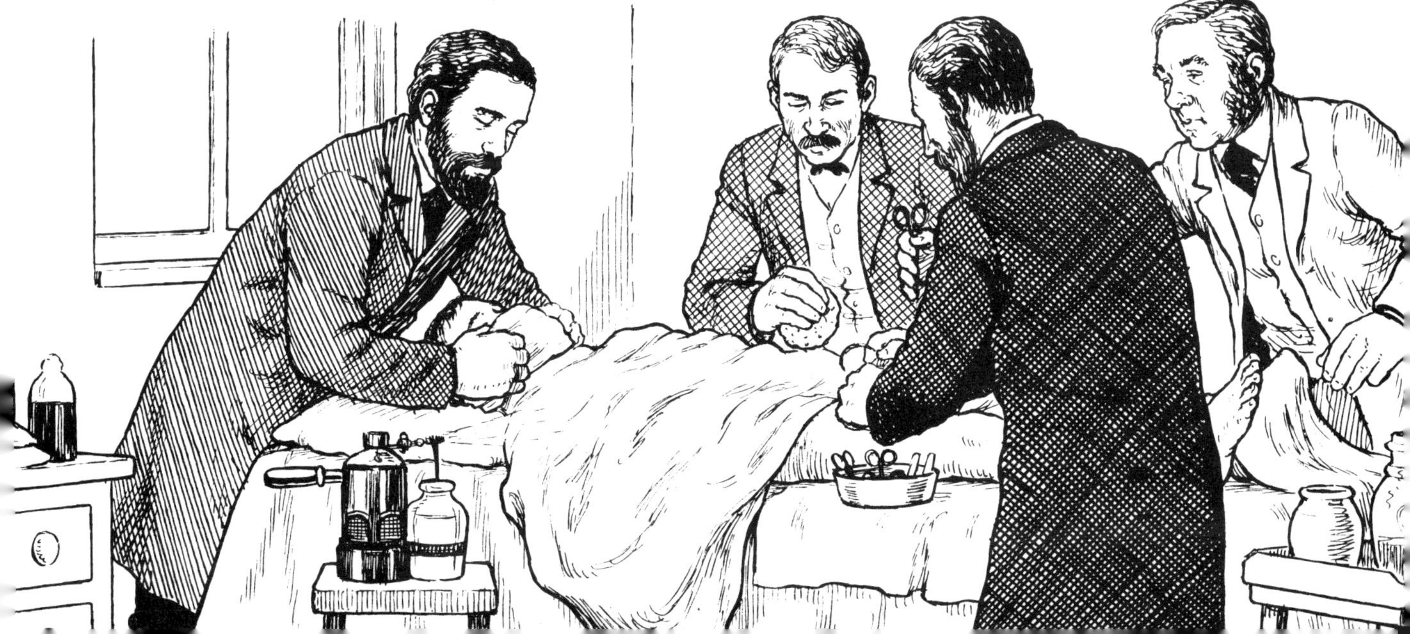

Malaria

PATRICK MANSON (1844—1922)
RONALD ROSS (1857—1932)

Malaria is the greatest killer of all the diseases that afflict mankind. Some estimates state that more than 5 billion people have died from its effects. That is more than the present day population of the entire world. It is now, more or less, restricted to the sub-tropical and tropical parts of the world, especially South America, Africa and India, but it was not always so. It was not uncommon in England in the Middle Ages and very common until recent years in southern Europe — Italy, Greece and parts of Spain. One of the difficulties in dealing with it was that people didn't know what caused it and how it was carried from one person to another. It was thought to be caused by the air rising from the swamps. People noticed that it was always more common in swampy areas and indeed the word malaria is from the Italian 'mal' — bad, and 'aria' — air.

A big step forward was taken in 1880 when the famous French biologist, Alphonse Laveran, showed malaria was caused by a little living organism that could be seen only under the microscope. This little organism, which he called 'Plasmodium', multiplied in the blood and entered and burst the red blood cells in humans, causing fever. But it still was not known how this little organism, the malarial parasite, passed from one person to another — how people who had malaria passed it on to other people.

Patrick Manson was born in Old Meldrum near Aberdeen, and after qualifying as a doctor at the University of Aberdeen, he went to China to look after the sick in the Baptist Missionary Society's hospital and later at the Seaman's Hospital. While in China he became interested in the terrible disease called elephantiasis which causes great swelling of arms, legs and other parts of the body. He found little thread-like worms called filaria in the blood of people who had the disease and he showed that these were passed or transmitted from person to person by the bite of a mosquito. When he moved on to Hong Kong he founded a College of Medicine to train students. He became famous for his knowledge of tropical diseases and was known as the 'Father of Tropical Medicine'. He became very interested in malaria too.

When he returned home to Britain he met a young medical officer, Ronald Ross, of Scottish descent, who was serving in the Indian Army. Ross was born in India, where his father was a General in the Indian Army, and he too was interested in how malaria was transmitted. Manson suggested to him that it might be by mosquitoes, so Ross hurried back to India to investigate. Manson arranged for him to work in Calcutta where he had the use of a laboratory. Birds can get a kind of malaria and since they were easier to work with than human patients, Ross investigated bird malaria and showed clearly that it was readily passed on from one bird to another by the bite of a mosquito. He also found the malaria parasites in the mosquito's stomach. He made beautiful drawings of all that he saw and in his report he stated that human malaria was also transmitted by the bite of mosquitoes. Unfortunately he had not proved it absolutely. An Italian biologist, called Grassi, claimed that he and not Ross was the first to do so. Ross accused Grassi of stealing his work.

Most of the great scientists and medical men of the time seemed to agree that Ross should be given credit for the discovery and he received the Nobel Prize for Medicine in 1902.

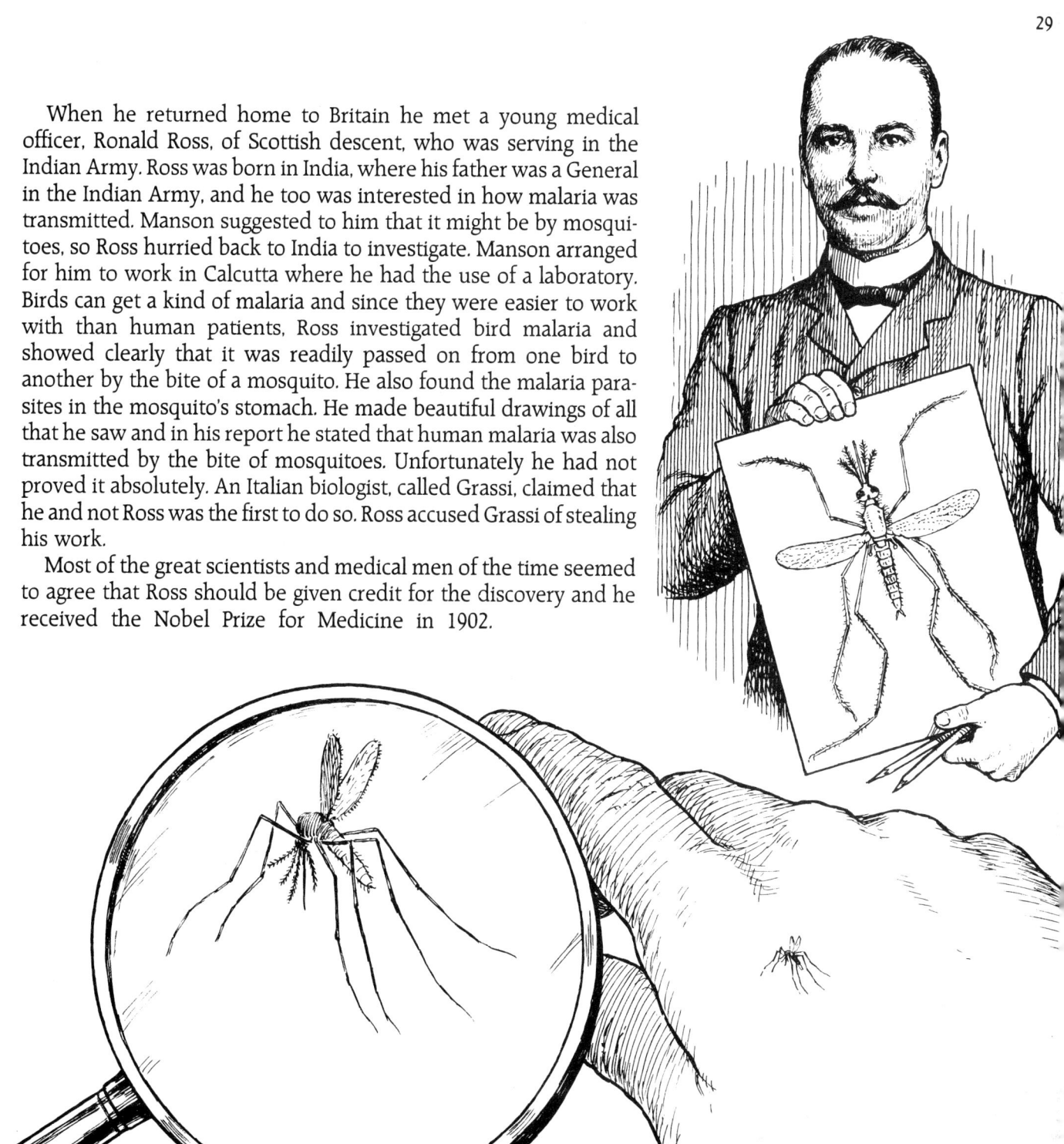

Penicillin
ALEXANDER FLEMING (1881–1955)

Alexander Fleming was born in Darvel, Ayrshire where his father was a farmer. Every week-day, as a little boy, Alex walked two miles over the moor to the little one-classroom Louden school. In midwinter when the icy winds blew, his mother would give him two hot potatoes 'in their jackets' to keep his hands warm as he walked and to provide him with a hot meal when he arrived at the school.

The Flemings were not rich and when Alex was only 14 he left his beloved moors to join his brothers, Tom a doctor and John an optician, in London. Alex got a job as a shipping clerk, for which he was paid about 2p an hour! His sister Mary moved down to London to look after her brothers. This was quite a common Scottish practice in those days. When Mary got married, her younger sister Grace took her place; and when Grace married, she was succeeded, to the boys' delight, by their beloved mother.

Alex worked for five years as a clerk, but when an uncle in Ayrshire died and left him £250, his brothers persuaded him to study medicine. After attending evening classes, he entered St Mary's Hospital, London, where he won many prizes and medals, including the Gold Medal of the University of London. When he graduated, it is not surprising that he was taken on to the staff at St Mary's.

When war broke out with Germany in 1914, he went to France as a medical officer. One thing that distressed him greatly was the enormous number of soldiers who died through fairly simple wounds becoming infected with germs. Once the germs got into the blood there was not a great deal that could be done to stop them — even cutting off infected arms and legs didn't seem to stop their progress. Indeed the greatest medical problem facing mankind was infection by germs, not only in wartime, but in peacetime too. The wards of the hospitals of the world were filled with patients suffering from blood poisoning because their wounds became infected after surgery. Also the infectious diseases such as pneumonia, diphtheria, scarlet fever, typhoid and many more were responsible for millions of deaths. Doctors could do little to help.

In the summer of 1928, in his laboratory in St Mary's, Fleming was examining plates on which he was growing some blood poisoning

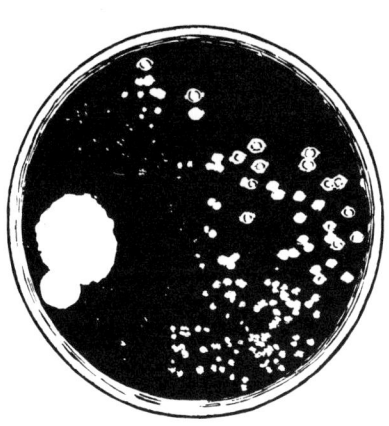

germs. Then he noticed a curious thing. On one of the plates there was a mould growing and all around the mould there was a clear area with no germs. He identified the mould as 'Penicillium' and he showed that it was giving out a 'juice' which prevented the germs from multiplying. He called the juice penicillin. The remarkable thing about penicillin was that, although it stopped germs from growing, it was completely harmless to humans. Surprisingly, Fleming did not try out penicillin on any of his patients, but he did publish a number of scientific papers about it.

Ten years later two doctors at Oxford, Howard Florey and Ernest Chain, started to look again at penicillin. They purified it and showed that when injected into patients suffering from 'blood poisoning' caused by certain germs, it cured them within a few days. Soon all the major chemical companies were producing penicillin. It was a wonder drug.

Fleming, Florey and Chain were all knighted and the three shared the Nobel Prize for Medicine in 1945. Honours came to Sir Alexander from all parts of the world, but the thing that gave him the greatest pleasure was a letter from an old lady in South Africa.

Dear little Alex,

Please forgive me — but you were about 8 or 9 years of age at most when I knew you — a dear little boy with dreamy blue eyes. This letter is just to congratulate my dear little friend of many moons ago and tell him that I have been following his career and rejoicing in all his wonderful successes.

Marion Stirling

Marion Stirling had been his teacher in the little moorland school.

Places to Visit

Birmingham: Museum of Science and Industry, Newhall Street.
New James Watt building has exhibits relating to him, and to
Boulton and Murdoch, including — the world's oldest working
steam engine; Murdoch's original steam carriage; and many of
Watt's inventions, including a copying machine.

Edinburgh: Royal Museum of Scotland, Chambers Street.
Exhibits include working models of early steam engines; model
of Murdoch's steam carriage; Watt engines; Baird TV receiver;
Dunlop's first tyre.

Glasgow: Hunterian Museum, University of Glasgow.
Permanent exhibits relating to Watt and Lord Kelvin.

Glasgow: Museum of Transport, Albert Drive.
Locomotives; ship models; model of Macmillan's bicycle.

Glasgow: People's Palace, Glasgow Green.
Organ built by Watt. Nearby in Glasgow Green is a stone
marking the spot where he hit on the idea of a separate
condenser.

Glasgow: University of Strathclyde.
Apparatus used by Baird is on display in the foyer of Baird Hall,
Sauchiehall Street. Manuscripts and instruments of Baird and
John Anderson can be seen by contacting the Curator, Collins
Exhibition Centre, off George Street.

Grangemouth: Museum, Bo'ness Road.
Exhibits relating to canals and to the 'Charlotte Dundas'.

Grangemouth: BP Information Centre.
Start of car trail tracing the life of 'Paraffin' Young and the
development of the shale oil industry.

London: Science Museum, South Kensington.
Exhibits relating to most of the people covered in this book;
special galleries include Telecommunications and the History of
Medicine. Teachers planning visits can obtain material
beforehand from the Education Officer.

Ayrshire Tour

Livingstone Centre: From Glasgow, take M73 then M74. Leave at Junction
5. Through Bothwell to Blantyre.

Fleming (memorial, farm and school): From Blantyre, take A724 to
Strathaven, from where A71 leads to Darvel.

Murdoch (house, mill and cave where he did early experiments): From
Darvel, take Kilmarnock Road A71. Just before Kilmarnock, take A76
through Mauchline to Cumnock.

Macadam (memorial park in Ayr; road and house in Sauchrie): From
Cumnock, take A70 to Ayr. From Ayr, go south on B7024 for about
5 miles. Turn right for Sauchrie on unnumbered road.

Dunlop (birthplace): From Sauchrie, return to Ayr. Take road through
Prestwick to Irvine A79. Just before Irvine, take A71 to Dreghorn.

Kelvin (house 'Netherhall' with plaque): From Dreghorn, return to Irvine
road, then continue north on coast road to Largs.

Young (grave and church): From Largs, continue north on coast road to
Inverkip.

Watt (McLean Museum and Art Gallery, Greenock — special exhibits): From
Inverkip, take A742 to Greenock.

Bell ('Comet' replica): From Greenock, take A8 to Port Glasgow.

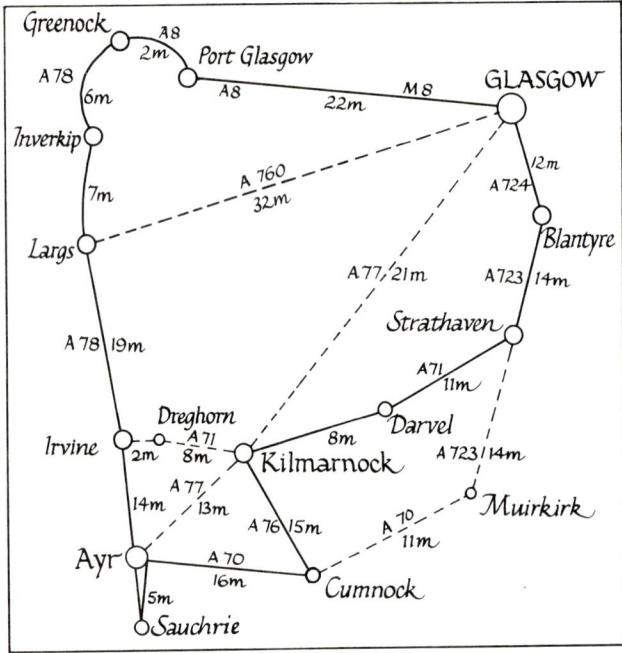

Acknowledgments

I am especially grateful to my wife, Elizabeth, and to my editor, Antony
Kamm, for their practical help and encouragement. My thanks are also due
to: Sir Samuel Curran; Ross Finlay; Jack House; Dr J A McFadzean; Professor
W W Macdonald; Murdoch Macpherson; Isobel Robertson; John Robertson;
Ayr Public Library; Birmingham Museum of Science and Industry;
BP Information Centre, Grangemouth; Livingston Development Corporation;
Mitchell Library, Glasgow; Science Museum, London; Scottish Development
Agency.

Bill Fletcher